J. R. R. TOLKIEN

Epic Fantasy Author

Eric Braun

LERNER PUBLICATIONS ◆ MINNEAPOLIS

Lerner Publications Company
An imprint of Lerner Publishing Group, Inc.
241 First Avenue North
Minneapolis, MN 55401 USA

For reading levels and more information, look up this title at www.lernerbooks.com.

Image credits: Time Life Pictures/Getty Images, p. 2; Haywood Magee/Picture Post/Hulton Archive/Getty Images, pp. 6, 8; Robert Harris/Wellcome Library, p. 10; Mabel Tolkien/Wikipedia Commons PD, p. 11; PA Images/Alamy Stock Photo, pp. 12, 27; Oosoom/English Wikipedia (CC BY-SA 3.0), p. 13; Special Collections at the University of Arizona Library Special Collections via Wikipedia Commons, p. 15; Southwick Codex/The British Library, p. 16; The Victoria Studio/ Wikipedia Commons, p. 17; Allan Baxter/Getty Images, p. 18; John Warwick Brooke/Wikipedia Commons, p. 20; Everett Collection/Alamy Stock Photo, p. 21; Sagarjethani/Wikipedia Commons (CC BY-SA 3.0), p. 23; CBW/Alamy Stock Photo, p. 25; D. Pimborough/Shutterstock.com, p. 28; neftali/Shutterstock.com, p. 30; AP Photo/Sang Tan, p. 32; Alpha Historica/Alamy Stock Photo, pp. 33, 39; Nick Savage/Alamy Stock Photo, p. 34; Eeli Purola/Shutterstock.com, p. 35; AP Photo, p. 36; AP Photo/Mark J. Terrill, p. 37; The Army Museum, Sweden, p. 38; Colin Underhill/Alamy Stock Photo, p. 40. Cover image: Haywood Magee/Getty Images.

Main body text set in Rotis Serif Std 55. Typeface provided by Adobe Systems.

Editor: Alison Lorenz **Designer:** Lauren Cooper **Photo Editor:** Cynthia Zemlicka
Lerner team: Sue Marquis

Library of Congress Cataloging-in-Publication Data

Names: Braun, Eric, 1971– author.
Title: J. R. R. Tolkien : epic fantasy author / Eric Braun.
Description: Minneapolis : Lerner Publications, 2022 | Series: Gateway biographies | Includes
    bibliographical references and index. | Audience: Ages 9–14 | Audience: Grades 4–6 |
    Summary: "The robust, imaginative works of J. R. R. Tolkien have sparked the imaginations
    of readers around the world. From World War I soldier to bestselling author, trace the life of
    the man behind Middle Earth"– Provided by publisher.
Identifiers: LCCN 2020025835 (print) | LCCN 2020025836 (ebook) | ISBN 9781728404479
    (library binding) | ISBN 9781728418186 (ebook)
Subjects: LCSH: Tolkien, J. R. R. (John Ronald Reuel), 1892–1973–Biography–Juvenile
    literature. | Authors, English–20th century–Biography–Juvenile literature.
Classification: LCC PR6039.O32 Z586 2022 (print) | LCC PR6039.O32 (ebook) | DDC 823/.912
    [B]–dc23

LC record available at https://lccn.loc.gov/2020025835
LC ebook record available at https://lccn.loc.gov/2020025836

Manufactured in the United States of America
1-48505-49019-4/19/2021

TABLE OF CONTENTS

J. R. R. Tolkien in his office at
Oxford University in 1955

It had been a long, busy day for Professor Tolkien. Early in the morning he and his sons had taken their bikes to Mass at St. Aloysius Catholic Church. After breakfast, he went to his office at Oxford University. He gave a lecture on *Beowulf*, an epic poem in Old English on which he was a well-known expert. He attended a meeting of the English faculty and worked on lecture notes for his upcoming classes. After helping his children with their homework, he attended another meeting at the college. Then, after dinner, he met with friends to translate and discuss Icelandic literature. When he returned home, he found his family all asleep.

It was late and Tolkien was tired. But he stoked the fire in the stove in his study and took out a manuscript he'd been working on. It was a children's story and not as serious as other stories he'd written. But even so, he felt pulled back to it each night. It charmed him. Even better, it seemed to charm his sons, Michael, Christopher, and John.

Tolkien wrote his famous fantasies, *The Hobbit* and *The Lord of the Rings*, while working as a professor.

Tolkien had always read or invented stories for his children in the evenings. Lately, he had been telling them a new story about Bilbo Baggins, who was a hobbit. What was a hobbit? Tolkien was learning himself as he wrote Bilbo's story. Hobbits were a lot like humans, and even a lot like Tolkien himself. They were simple people who liked good food, friendships, and the natural world. But unlike Tolkien, they were short—about half the size of the average human.

"The Hobbits are just rustic English people, made small in size because it reflects the generally small reach of their imagination—not the small reach of their courage or latent power," he explained years later.

That night in his study, the hobbits kept him up late. He wrote the next chapter in Bilbo's story on the backs of student essays. Tolkien didn't know it then, but these nights working on the hobbit story for his children would change his life. He had written stories before, many of which involved a mythology he was inventing—a world full of wizards, dwarves, elves, and magic. But he had also abandoned many stories before they were complete. It took many years for Tolkien to understand how hobbits fit into his mythology and for him to finish the story.

When he did, Tolkien's creation didn't change only his life. *The Hobbit* and its sequel, *The Lord of the Rings*, changed the world. The stories created a new mythology that to millions of readers feels as authentic as the ancient mythologies that inspired it. From a seemingly unserious children's story, Tolkien created an epic world.

A Childhood in Nature

Many years earlier, John Ronald Reuel Tolkien's parents, Arthur Tolkien and Mabel Suffield, had fallen in love and wanted to get married. But Tolkien's family had gone bankrupt, and he didn't have the money to support a family of his own. So Arthur Tolkien made a big move. He took a banking job in South Africa. South Africa was far away from England, and life there was very different. But prospectors there were finding gold and diamonds, and banking was a booming business.

The move paid off. Arthur Tolkien made a good living in South Africa. Suffield joined him in March of 1891, and the two were married the following month. They settled in the town of Bloemfontein. On January 3, 1892, their first child was born. They named him John Ronald Reuel Tolkien and called him Ronald.

As a young boy, Ronald spent a lot of time in his family's garden. But it was often too hot to be outside. The heat seemed to affect Ronald's health, as he tended to get fevers. His mother disliked the oppressive climate and longed to move back to England. But his father's bank was doing well, so they stayed. Ronald's brother, Hilary, was born in February 1894.

A diamond mine in Bultfontein, South Africa, in 1888

The Tolkiens' 1892 Christmas card shows a baby John Ronald Reuel (*right*).

In April 1895 Mabel Tolkien took Ronald and Hilary on a long visit to England. Arthur Tolkien stayed behind to attend to business. Staying for several months with her family in Birmingham, Ronald's health improved. But that fall his mother received a message from South Africa. Arthur Tolkien had rheumatic fever. When his condition got worse, she decided to take the boys home. Ronald dictated a letter to his father, telling him how excited he was to see him. But Arthur Tolkien never saw the letter. He died on February 15, 1896.

With no job and little money, Mabel Tolkien decided she and her sons would continue to stay with her parents in Birmingham. Over time, Ronald began to feel closer to his grandparents and the rest of his mother's family. But the home was cramped with so many people living there. In the summer of 1896, she moved with her boys to their own home, a small cottage just outside the hamlet of Sarehole.

Living in the English
countryside sparked Ronald's
imagination. He and his brother explored a corn mill
and a quiet pond where swans lived. They explored a
bog and wooded hills, scenes that would later appear in
Ronald's stories. The brothers often ventured onto other
people's land to pick mushrooms, only to be chased
away by angry farmers. Many years later, Hilary Tolkien
remembered those days fondly. "We spent lovely summers
just picking flowers and trespassing," he said.

Ronald spent much of his time outside. His mother
gave him lessons in botany, and he developed a special

fondness for trees. He also loved to draw, especially the wonders he saw in nature. He filled pages with his drawings of landscapes and trees.

Ronald loved language even more. He could read by the time he was four. He began to learn Latin and French. His affinity for words extended to stories, especially adventure stories. *The Red Fairy Book* by Andrew Lang was his favorite book. One story in the book told of a character who fought a dragon. Ronald read it over and over. He became fascinated by dragons, and when he was seven years old, he wrote his own dragon story.

The Tolkiens' first home in Birmingham, near Sarehole Mill and Moseley Bog

In 1900, when Ronald was eight, he started school at King Edward's, the same school his father had attended as a boy. It was 4 miles (6 km) away, in Birmingham, so Mabel Tolkien and the boys moved back there.

The move was a harsh transition. Their home in the city was in a busy neighborhood, a far cry from the idyllic surroundings in Sarehole. Ronald found it miserable. But he liked school and began to excel. Two years later, Mabel Tolkien, who had converted to Catholicism, transferred the boys to a Catholic school that was more affordable than King Edward's. She and the boys moved again to be closer to their new school. But her conversion angered her Protestant family, and from then on they cut her off financially.

At the St Philip's Grammar School, Mabel Tolkien and the boys became good friends with a priest, the Reverend Francis Xavier Morgan. His friendship was deeply important to the family. When Mabel Tolkien died of diabetes in 1904, Morgan became the boys' legal guardian.

A Young Man's Loves

By the time his mother died, Ronald had returned again to King Edward's School after winning a scholarship. He continued to excel in his studies, especially in languages.

Ronald studied Latin, Greek, and German. He loved the Middle English of Chaucer's *Canterbury Tales*. He also began to study philology, the study of language. He was fascinated with the structure of language, how it worked, how it developed over time, and how different languages related to one another. With the encouragement of one of his teachers, he began to study Old English, the earliest historical form of the English language. Eventually he was able to read the epic poem *Beowulf* in its original Old English. The poem tells of a warrior who fights monsters and a dragon.

In those years, Ronald and Hilary spent many holidays with their relatives. Their cousins Mary and Marjorie Incledon had invented their own language called Animalic. Ronald, with his deep passion for languages, was intrigued and inspired. He soon began inventing his

A page from *Beowulf*,
written in Old English

own, including one that was based on the ancient Gothic language.

In 1908 Morgan moved Ronald and Hilary to a boardinghouse in Birmingham. The other boarder in the building was Edith Bratt. Like Ronald and Hilary, Bratt was an orphan. Though she was nineteen and Ronald was sixteen, the two became close friends. They rode bikes together, went to tea together, and even invented a secret whistle to call to each other.

Eventually, Morgan found out about Ronald's relationship with Bratt. He instructed Ronald not to see her again until he reached the age of twenty-one. Ronald loved his guardian, and he was dependent on him for money. So he did what he was told. But over the following weeks, he was depressed and lonely.

During his final year at King Edward's School, Ronald and some of his close friends began having tea secretly in the library. That summer they shifted teatime to Barrow Stores, a department store and café near the school. Ronald and three others formed a semisecret club that they called the T.C.B.S., or Tea Club, Barrovian Society. All the boys were excellent scholars and lovers of Latin and Greek literature and poetry.

In the summer of 1911, Ronald and Hilary joined a group of friends on a vacation to Switzerland, where they set out on a walking trip. Carrying packs of supplies, the group hiked and camped across the mountains. The views Ronald saw there became the inspiration for the Misty Mountains, across which Bilbo Baggins would journey in *The Hobbit.*

That fall Tolkien went to college at Oxford University. At first, he studied classics, or topics such as ancient Greek and Roman culture, but then he changed his focus to English language and literature. January 3, 1913, was his twenty-first birthday. Having fulfilled his promise to his guardian, Tolkien wrote to Bratt to say that he still loved her. He asked her to marry him, but when she wrote back, she said she was engaged to someone else.

Tolkien went to visit Bratt in Cheltenham, where she was living. She met him at the train station, and they spent the day talking. She told Tolkien that she wanted to marry him, and she broke off her engagement to the other man.

Tolkien returned to Oxford, where he was busy with rugby, boating, debating, and expanding his passion for language. In 1914 he wrote a poem "The Voyage of Éarendel the Evening Star," about a mariner who takes his ship into the sky and sails among the stars. This scene became the beginning of the mythology that would make up the world of *The Hobbit* and *The Lord of the Rings*.

Oxford University

That summer World War I (1914–1918) began and England declared war on Germany.

In the fall Tolkien entered his final year at Oxford and also began to train for the army. He kept up with his usual schoolwork while he drilled with the Officers' Training Corps. Tolkien thrived under the busy conditions. Over Christmas he met with his friends in the T.C.B.S., with whom he was still close.

After the meeting, Tolkien began to write more poetry, including sequels to the "Éarendel" poem. He completed his degree in the summer of 1915, and in March 1916, he and Bratt married.

World War I

In June 1916 Tolkien received his orders from the army. He was headed to France, where he would serve in the Battle of the Somme as a second lieutenant.

The Battle of the Somme was a huge offensive by the British and French against the Germans along the River Somme. More than three million people participated in the battle, and over a third of them were killed or injured. As Tolkien marched into battle, he saw dead and wounded men everywhere. Even trees had been stripped and burned to blackened trunks. Back at home, his wife was plagued with worry.

But Tolkien had many health issues during the war and was often removed from combat to heal. In October he

British soldiers in a trench during the Battle of the Somme in 1916

contracted trench fever, a serious infection carried by lice. While he recovered back in England, most of his battalion was killed. In the hospital at the end of the year, Tolkien learned that all but one of his friends from his beloved T.C.B.S. had been killed in the war too.

Tolkien spent the rest of the war either recovering in hospitals or working in noncombat roles. During this downtime he began work on a book called "The Book of Lost Tales." Tolkien had always wanted to invent languages, but he felt that languages must have history.

"The Book of Lost Tales" was Tolkien's attempt to record that history.

One story in the book was "The Fall of Gondolin." The story described an evil being, Morgoth, leading an attack against Gondolin, a city inhabited by elves. Among the elves in Gondolin is Éarendel, the protagonist of Tolkien's earlier poem and the grandson of the king. The names Tolkien created for his characters and places were all formed from his invented languages. Some have suggested that the heroic battle scene in "The Fall of Gondolin" was Tolkien's reaction to the gruesome fighting he witnessed at the Somme.

Land destroyed by bombs and fighting in World War I

Another story in the book was inspired by his wife. Every so often Tolkien could go on leave from the military, and they went walking in the countryside. On one such walk, she sang and danced in the woods. The moment inspired the story of Beren, a mortal man who loves the immortal elf Lúthien Tinúviel, whom he first sees dancing in the woods.

Tolkien never finished "The Book of Lost Tales," though many of its stories later made up the core of another work, *The Silmarillion*. They also formed the foundation of the mythology within *The Hobbit* and *The Lord of the Rings*.

STARTING A CAREER

The couple's first son, John Francis Reuel Tolkien, was born on November 16, 1917. His middle name was in honor of the Reverend Francis Xavier Morgan, who had cared for Tolkien when he was younger. The priest came from Birmingham to baptize the baby.

World War I ended on November 11, 1918, but Tolkien still had to complete his term in the army. He asked to be stationed near Oxford, and his request was granted. The Tolkiens and Edith Tolkien's cousin Jennie Grove found a home there. At last, Tolkien and his family could live together.

Tolkien found a job with the New English Dictionary, where he researched the history of words. Experts had been compiling the dictionary since 1879. The work was pleasing to Tolkien, and he was good at it. Researching how a simple word such as *wasp* had changed in meaning and pronunciation—and looking at comparable words in old and ancient languages such as Old Saxon, Middle Dutch, and Latin—fit his talents and passions perfectly. "I learned more in those two years than in any other equal period of my life," he later said.

In the fall of 1920 Tolkien accepted a job at the University of Leeds as reader of English, a position just below full professor. Leeds was in northern England, and Tolkien moved there alone. His wife was pregnant at the time, and she gave birth to their second son, Michael Hilary Reuel Tolkien, on October 22. Tolkien was able to see

Tolkien's home in Leeds, England

his family only when he traveled back to Oxford on weekends. But in early 1921 his wife and boys joined him in Leeds.

At Leeds, Tolkien's reputation grew. He published *A Middle English Vocabulary* and, along with his friend E. V. Gordon, an edition of *Sir Gawain and the Green Knight*, which they translated from Old English. Tolkien was promoted to professor in 1924.

The Tolkiens' third child, Christopher John Reuel Tolkien, was born in November 1924. The following year, Tolkien applied for and won the position of professor of Anglo-Saxon at Oxford. The family moved again.

THE OXFORD YEARS

Back in Oxford, Tolkien and his family settled into a comfortable life. They bought a small house in North Oxford, a suburban area that was home to many academics and their families. Tolkien rode his bike to school, church, shops, and anywhere else he needed to go in town. In 1929 their fourth child, Priscilla Mary Anne Reuel Tolkien, was born.

Tolkien was an expert on literature in Old and Middle English, and he had a special fondness for *Beowulf*, the epic poem he had first read as a schoolboy. He spent much of his time in the 1920s working on a new translation of the poem. His lectures on the piece were well-loved. Professor Tolkien would walk into the room and, without introduction, begin to loudly and dramatically recite the poem's opening lines in the original Old English.

As Tolkien settled into a routine of teaching, lecturing, attending meetings, and spending time with his family, he was able to devote more time to his personal writing. The imaginary world he wanted to create—that mythical history behind his invented languages—was never far from his mind. He had created a universe, Eä, which held several worlds, including Middle-Earth, where his later works would be set. He called the poems and prose that concerned this universe *The Silmarillion.*

Many pieces in *The Silmarillion* focused on the story of Beren and Lúthien,

Though Tolkien wrote pieces of *The Silmarillion* before *The Hobbit*, the work wasn't published until after his death.

which had become central to the telling of Eä. In 1926 Tolkien wrote "Sketch of the Mythology," a twenty-eight-page summary of his invented universe. He sent the "Sketch" and several poems to R. W. Reynolds, a teacher of his at King Edward's School. Reynolds was not particularly impressed with the pieces that dealt with Eä's mythology, though he did like some of Tolkien's other material. But Tolkien remained committed to his mythology.

Though the story of Eä was Tolkien's main focus, he also wrote stories to tell his children. Since his oldest son, John, was little, Tolkien had told him stories to help him sleep at night. Early stories featured a boy named Carrots who climbed into a cuckoo clock, leading to many strange adventures. Later stories involved a dog named Rover, inspired by a toy dog John lost on a beach. When Michael had nightmares, Tolkien told him stories about Bill Stickers, a big, troublesome character who always got away with mischief.

Tolkien's kids loved his stories and kept asking for more. Tolkien was happy to keep them coming, though not all his stories were successful. Many he abandoned. Others, such as the tale of the mysterious old forest dweller Tom Bombadil, showed up in later works. In 1934 Tolkien published the poem "The Adventures of Tom Bombadil" in *Oxford Magazine*. Bombadil also showed up in *The Lord of the Rings*.

In addition to writing stories, Tolkien was drawing and painting. He didn't consider himself a good artist, but he created elaborate full-color illustrations for one of his children's stories, "Mr. Bliss," about a tall, thin man who lives in a tall, thin house, and has many mishaps driving his car.

Each year around Christmas, Tolkien composed elaborate letters from Father Christmas to his children. The letters were illustrated and told stories about what had happened at the North Pole that year. Characters such as a polar bear who lived with Father Christmas and a

Priscilla Tolkien with her father's drawing of Bag End, the home of *The Hobbit*'s Bilbo Baggins, in 2004

snowman who worked as his gardener were featured in these annual stories. On each envelope Tolkien placed a North Pole postage stamp that he hand-painted. Then he left the envelopes for the kids to find.

THERE LIVED A HOBBIT

Sometime in the early 1930s the world of Tolkien's *Silmarillion* crashed into the world of his children's stories, though he didn't realize it at first. While grading student essays, he came across a blank sheet of paper in a student's exam book. On the page he wrote, "In a hole in the ground there lived a hobbit." Where did the sentence come from? Why did he write it? Later, he wrote: "I did not and do not know why."

The Hobbit
or There and Back Again

J. R. R. TOLKIEN

Illustrated by the Author

Since its publication, *The Hobbit* has sold over one hundred million copies.

But Tolkien was curious to find out more about the hobbit—whatever it was. He began to build a story around the sentence. Hobbits were humanlike but half the size of humans. They lived in underground houses built into the sides of hills, and they farmed and gardened. The hobbit in this sentence, the protagonist of Tolkien's growing story, was Bilbo Baggins.

Tolkien initially abandoned the story, only to return to it again. And he gave up on it more than once. Still, when he completed chapters, he read them to his sons, who thought the story was great. But Tolkien struggled to write the ending. As the boys grew older, they didn't ask for stories as often. The tale of Bilbo Baggins languished.

The story might never have been finished if not for one of Tolkien's former students, Elaine Griffiths. Griffiths occasionally did work for London publisher Allen & Unwin. After seeing Tolkien's manuscript, Griffiths suggested that her friend, an editor named Susan Dagnall, ask Tolkien for a look. Dagnall read Tolkien's story and thought it was good enough to consider for publication—it just needed an ending.

By October 1936, *The Hobbit* was finally completed, and Tolkien sent it to Allen & Unwin for their consideration. Since it was a children's book, Stanley Unwin asked his ten-year-old son to read it and report back. The boy's report was positive. "This book, with help of maps, does not need any illustrations it is good and should appeal to all children between the ages of 5 and 9," he wrote. The company agreed to publish the book.

Tolkien included over one hundred illustrations with *The Hobbit* manuscript that he submitted to his publisher. Some of them later appeared on stamps.

The Hobbit begins when Bilbo Baggins is visited by a wizard, Gandalf, and a band of dwarves. Gandalf convinces Baggins to join them on a mission to the Lonely Mountain to slay the dragon Smaug. The group encounters trolls, goblins, giant spiders, and evil wolves called wargs on their journey. They cross the Misty Mountains, a landscape inspired by Tolkien's trek across Switzerland years before. Baggins also discovers a mysterious ring that makes him invisible. The story shows Baggins experiencing enormous personal growth in accessing his deepest courage and wits.

Writing an Epic

The Hobbit received mostly good reviews, including a particularly good one from the author C. S. Lewis, who had become close friends with Tolkien. "All who love that kind of children's book which can be read and re-read by adults should take note that a new star has appeared in that constellation," Lewis said. When the book was published in the United States a few months later by Houghton Mifflin, it received similarly strong reviews. The *New York Herald Tribune* awarded *The Hobbit* its prize for best juvenile book of the season.

The Inklings

At Oxford, Tolkien became close friends with C. S. Lewis, a fellow professor and writer. Lewis would go on to write *The Chronicles of Narnia* among other works. Around the time Tolkien began work on *The Hobbit*, he and Lewis began meeting regularly with a group of writers to read and discuss one another's works. The group called themselves the Inklings. The group's meetings were casual, but they were important to Tolkien and he rarely missed one. He shared chapters of *The Lord of the Rings* with the men.

The first edition of *The Hobbit*,
published in 1937

The first print run of the book sold out before the end of the year, and Tolkien's publishers rushed to print more. *The Hobbit* was a hit, and Unwin began to ask Tolkien about his next book. Tolkien submitted several of his children's stories, including those featuring Mr. Bliss and Rover, but while Unwin liked them, he wanted something starring hobbits. Tolkien gave him *The Silmarillion*, but the publisher turned it down as well. Tolkien was determined to write something new—something that would be a proper sequel to *The Hobbit*.

When he wrote *The Hobbit*, Tolkien did not think it fit into the universe of *The Silmarillion*. But as he considered his sequel, it became clear that it did. In fact, hobbits were an important part of the stories of Middle-Earth. Their courage was at its core. The difference was that the story of Bilbo Baggins was set much later than those in *The Silmarillion*. Tolkien decided that *The Silmarillion* focused on the First and Second Ages of Middle-Earth. *The Hobbit*,

J. R. R. Tolkien

he realized, was
a story from the
Third Age.
Bilbo Baggins had
completed his adventure in *The
Hobbit*, so Tolkien could not put Bilbo at the center of his
new book. Instead, he decided, it would be Bilbo's nephew,
Bingo. Through the end of 1937 and early 1938, he
began writing notes about the new story and an opening
chapter. He sent the chapter to Unwin's son to read. The
boy liked it, and the publisher told Tolkien he should
proceed with this story.

Tolkien changed Bingo's name to Frodo and homed
in on the ring from *The Hobbit* as a key part of the
story. The dark lord Sauron—who had appeared in *The
Hobbit* as the Necromancer—was searching for the ring.

A letter from Tolkien to
Rayner Unwin, his editor
at Allen & Unwin

70 SANDFIELD ROAD.
HEADINGTON.
OXFORD.
TELEPHONE: OXFORD 61699.

12. May, 1955.

Dear Rayner,

As Tolkien wrote,
the story grew,
becoming much
more complicated than
its predecessor. It also became darker and more clearly
connected to *The Silmarillion.* In the spring of 1938
Tolkien came up with the title: *The Lord of the Rings.*

The following fall World War II (1939–1945) broke
out, and Tolkien found his home life much quieter and
lonelier. John, his oldest son, had gone to Rome to
become a Catholic priest. Michael and Christopher had
gone to serve in the war. The only child still at home
was Priscilla.

Over the next few years, Tolkien worked on and off on
The Lord of the Rings. Progress was slow. The book had

become a massive, complicated, epic story, and Tolkien was a perfectionist. He wanted every detail to fit perfectly into the universe of *The Silmarillion.* The names of places and characters had to come organically from his invented languages.

Finally, in 1947, Tolkien completed the story. After several rounds of revisions, he turned it over to his publisher in the fall of 1949. Tolkien hoped to pressure Allen & Unwin into publishing *The Silmarillion* along with the new book, but they refused. The feud between author and the publisher led to a further delay in the book's publishing. It wasn't until 1954 that the first part of *The Lord of the Rings* was published as *The Fellowship of the Ring.* The second part, *The Two Towers*, came out later that year. The third and final installment, *The Return of the King*, came in 1955.

The Hobbit and *The Lord of the Rings* trilogy

Rayner Unwin, the boy who had read *The Hobbit* for his father's company as a ten-year-old, was now an editor working with Tolkien. It was his idea to break the book into three parts with separate titles in an attempt to get more review coverage—and because the story was so long.

CELEBRITY AUTHOR

The Lord of the Rings trilogy finally saw the light of day. The reviews were mixed—some were negative, but many were extremely positive. W. H. Auden, writing for the *New York Times,* called it an inspiration. Sales at first were sluggish, but they picked up over the years.

Tolkien's works were popular among counterculture movements in the 1960s. Fans were drawn to the author's obvious love of nature and hatred of war.

Tolkien On-Screen

Tolkien sold the stage and film rights to *The Hobbit* and *The Lord of the Rings* in 1968, but he never saw his books become movies. An animated musical version of *The Hobbit* came out as a television movie in 1977, four years after Tolkien's death. In the late 1970s two animated musical films depicted *The Lord of the Rings* on television. Between 2001 and 2003 *The Lord of the Rings* was released as a live-action trilogy directed by Peter Jackson. The films received great reviews, won many awards, and drew millions to theaters. Then, between 2012 and 2014, Jackson's *The Hobbit* was released as a trilogy. *Tolkien*, a biopic of the author's life, was released in 2019. As of 2021 a new television series set during the Second Age of Middle-Earth was in production.

Peter Jackson (*front*) accepts the Oscar for Best Picture for *The Lord of the Rings: The Return of the King* in 2004, as the movie's cast looks on.

Tolkien's works inspired dozens of adaptations, from TV shows and musicals to board games like this one.

Over time, it became clear that *The Lord of the Rings*, along with *The Hobbit*, should be considered classics. The deep history Tolkien had created, including the languages he'd invented, made readers feel as though they were not merely reading a story but entering a different world. Tolkien's stories tell readers that life is heroic, and that everyone can do great things.

In 1961 Tolkien was nominated for the Nobel Prize in Literature. His fame and wealth continued to grow for the rest of his life.

Tolkien retired in 1959, and fans and reporters sought him out regularly. To retain some privacy, he had his name removed from the phone book and he and his wife moved to Bournemouth, a seaside resort home to many in the British upper middle class. With

Tolkien around 1967

the wealth
that came
from his book
sales, the couple led
a comfortable life. They
enjoyed relaxing together and talking about their
family. For two orphans, the idea of having built their
own happy family was very important. Edith Tolkien
was especially happy in their new town.

Tolkien still wished to see *The Silmarillion*—his
collection of works about the universe of Eä—published,
and he continued to tinker with it, but never changed
it significantly.

In November 1971 Edith Tolkien became ill with an
inflamed gallbladder. She died on November 29. The loss

was crushing for Tolkien. He soon moved back to Oxford to be near his friends and the more intellectual life of the university. He spent time with his son Christopher and Christopher's family. Tolkien also visited Christopher Wiseman, his old friend from the T.C.B.S, and his brother, Hilary.

On August 28, 1973, Tolkien returned to Bournemouth to see friends. While there, he became ill and had to be taken to a hospital. He had a bleeding ulcer and the next day developed a chest infection. On September 2, a Sunday morning, he died.

The Tolkiens' headstone, engraved with the names Beren and Lúthien

EDITH MARY TOLKIEN
LUTHIEN
1889 - 1971
JOHN RONALD
REUEL TOLKIEN
BEREN
1892 - 1973

Over the following years, Tolkien's son Christopher pulled together the pieces of *The Silmarillion*. He sought out his father's most up-to-date drafts and notes and tried to build a coherent narrative by filling in gaps, correcting inconsistencies, and accounting for the events of *The Lord of the Rings*. The final product included an Elvish word list as well as maps and genealogies.

Finally, in 1977, *The Silmarillion* was published. The massive, sprawling universe that Tolkien first created half a century before was complete. It took time, but Tolkien created a world that would continue to inspire readers for generations.

Important Dates

1892   John Ronald Reuel Tolkien is born in Bloemfontein, South Africa, on January 3.

1896   His father, Arthur Tolkien, dies in February while Ronald is on a trip with his mother and brother, and the family moves to England.

1904   His mother dies in November.

1911   Ronald joins the T.C.B.S. at King Edward's School.

         He hikes across mountains in Switzerland in the summer and starts at Oxford in the fall.

1916   He and Edith Bratt are married on March 22.

         In June he leaves to fight in the Battle of the Somme.

         In November he returns to England with trench fever.

1917   He begins writing "The Book of Lost Tales," which eventually becomes *The Silmarillion*.

1930s	He begins writing *The Hobbit* but abandons it before it is finished.
1936	He finishes *The Hobbit*, and the book is accepted for publication.
1937	*The Hobbit* is published, and Tolkien begins working on *The Lord of the Rings*.
1954	The first volume in *The Lord of the Rings* trilogy is published.
1959	Tolkien retires.
1971	Edith Tolkien dies in November.
1973	Tolkien dies on September 2 at the age of eighty-one.
1977	*The Silmarillion* is published after being edited by Tolkien's son Christopher.
2017	Amazon announces it plans to release a new TV series based on Tolkien's works.

SOURCE NOTES

8 Humphrey Carpenter, *J.R.R. Tolkien: A Biography* (Boston: Houghton Mifflin, 2000), 180.

12 Carpenter, 28.

23 Carpenter, 108.

28 Carpenter, 181.

29 Carpenter, 184.

30–31 Carpenter, 186.

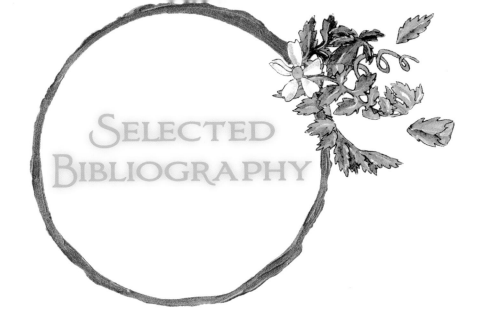

SELECTED BIBLIOGRAPHY

Carpenter, Humphrey. *J.R.R. Tolkien: A Biography.* Boston: Houghton Mifflin, 2000.

Doughan, David. "J.R.R. Tolkien: A Biographical Sketch." Tolkien Society. Last modified January 20, 2010. https://www.tolkiensociety.org/author/biography/.

Duriez, Colin. *J.R.R. Tolkien.* Blue Ash, OH: David & Charles, 2012.

"J.R.R. Tolkien Biography." Biography.com. Last modified September 11, 2019. https://www.biography.com/writer/jrr-tolkien.

"Tolkien Biography." Tolkien Library. Accessed January 27, 2021. http://www.tolkienlibrary.com/abouttolkien.htm.

LEARN MORE

BOOKS

Felix, Rebecca. *Peter Jackson: Director of* The Lord of the Rings *and* The Hobbit *Trilogies.* Minneapolis: Checkerboard Library, 2017.

Potter, William. *Epic Adventures.* New York: PowerKids, 2020.

Zamosky, Lisa. *World War I.* Huntington Beach, CA: Teacher Created Materials, 2019.

WEBSITES

Kiddle: J. R. R. Tolkien Facts for Kids
https://kids.kiddle.co/J._R._R._Tolkien

LOTR Project: Map of Middle-Earth
http://lotrproject.com/map/

Tolkien Gateway
http://tolkiengateway.net/wiki/Main_Page

INDEX